Reminders
FOR THE
Journey

Lynne,

From my "grateful"
heart to yours . . . .
thank you for
your valuable
assistance !

Sharon

Reminders
FOR THE
Journey

Sharon Anderson

Bridges
of Hope
PUBLISHING

Reminders for the Journey: Reflections for Mothers

Bridges of Hope Publishing
P.O. Box 407
South Easton, MA 02375

ISBN: 0-9642838-1-6

Library of Congress Catalog Card Number: 00-90060

Web site: www.bridgesofhope.com

10 9 8 7 6 5 4 3 2 1

This book is lovingly dedicated to

my precious mother,

Sally Jo Harff,

whose love,

support and encouragement

has followed me every day

of my life

Table of Contents

To contact Sharon Anderson
about speaking engagements,
write or call
Bridges of Hope
P.O. Box 407
South Easton, MA 02375
(508) 583-1555

Visit the Bridges of Hope web site
at www.bridgesofhope.com

Acknowledgments

Writing a book is much like giving birth. An idea is conceived. Long months of development follow. And then the joy of delivery. Throughout the process, you are supported and encouraged by an army of caregivers and cheerleaders. My heart is filled with gratitude to each of these "enablers" – my gifts from heaven.

My husband, Karl who is the mainstay of my life.

My "teachers" and children Katy, Amy, Brian, Rachel, Christy and Brad – whose uniqueness taught me how to be a better mother.

My illustrator and daughter, Katy, whose beautiful flowered illustrations enhance the message of this book.

My graphic artist and sister, Stephanie Carlson who designed a cover of creative excellence.

My assistant, Jill Hutchinson who has dedicated herself so steadfastly and competently to each component of this project.

My brother-in-law, Paul Anderson and my long-time acquaintance, Lynne Hopper who edited my work with expert precision to detail.

My family and friends – you know who you are – who fill my life not only with sweetness but substance as well.

From the Author

My youngest son went through a stage recently when he worried about everything. He even went as far as to worry about whether I was going to die one day when I went to bed with a bad headache. I felt terrible that he was so riddled with fear.

"Brad, I'm fine," I assured him. "I just have a migraine headache. I'll be good as new tomorrow." He was quiet for a minute so I probed further. "Why are you so worried that I'm going to die?"

With not a hint of hesitation, he scripted his memorable answer. "Because there is only one of you." Talk about a heart grabber!

There is definitely something about a mother's love to be sure. Something so strong, so deep, so enduring that it sets itself apart from all other forms of earthly love. Its capacity is endless. Its effect, life changing. It knows no bounds nor is it changed with age.

I don't know what it is. Maybe it's the nurturing aspect of motherhood that makes it so. The emotional, mental, and physical sustenance a mother provides day in and day out. Maybe it's the shelter of her presence. The protective shield she builds around her children. Or maybe it's the demonstrative role she plays. The hug when it's needed, the kiss to make it all better. Whatever it is, it's pure mother and it's pure gold.

I know people in their sixties who admit there are still days when they "miss their mother." When they wish she was around to say "everything will be all right" or "you did a great job" or "you are special to me." It seems a mother's love attaches itself to a child's heart and never lets go.

I've relished each aspect of my role as a mother through the years. I've enjoyed each and every stage of the journey. In fact, I consider it to be one of my highest callings, second only to my role as a wife. I've had quite an education at the hands of my six children. They have taught me a great deal about how to be a better mother, much of which I am passing on to you now.

It saddens me to see the way motherhood has been so trivialized in our culture today. Instead of a woman feeling worthwhile and respected in her role as a mother, she is often made to feel inferior and insignificant. It is time the value of motherhood be lifted up once again.

I'd like to think that is what *Reminders for the Journey* is all about. It brings to the forefront the significant role mothers play in the lives of their children while at the same time providing gentle reminders of the best kind. Wonderful child-raising principles that last a lifetime.

My prayer as you read this book is that you will remember, always remember, "there is only one of you."

You wake up in the morning, and lo!
your purse is magically filled
with twenty four hours of the
unmanufactured tissue of
the universe of life. It is yours.
It is the most precious
of possessions.
No one can take it
from you.
It is unstealable.
And no one receives either
more or less than you receive.

Arnold Bennett

Celebrate Today

While waiting in my doctor's office one afternoon, I read a story that touched my life in a very poignant way. It took place during a time when I was especially weary of dealing with the unending challenges of daily living. A time when I didn't feel like rejoicing about anything, let alone the promise of another day. Have you ever felt this way? If you are human (and honest), you know what I am talking about. Read with me the details of this moving story.

A minister, visiting an elderly man in the hospital, was drawn to the Children's Wing as he was searching for an exit. It was a medium-sized Mickey Mouse with a dazzling smile that beckoned him toward the room that was called "Children's Oncology Ward." As he looked through the window, he saw oxygen tanks, IV tubes, electronic monitoring devices and children with no hair, dark haunting circles surrounding their eyes, and skin color which was grayish or grayish yellow. As he stood there, he began to cry.

It was then that he felt a hand on his arm. It was a nun who said, "Is something wrong?" When she asked him if he wanted to talk, he nodded "Yes." Her name was Sister Maria. She wanted to know which of the children were his.

"None of them," he replied.

"Why does it hurt you so much when you see these children?" she asked.

"I don't like death," he responded.

"I've been working with these kinds of children everyday for the last fourteen years," she said.

"How can you stand working with death all the time?" he questioned.

Her simple answer dumbfounded him: "I don't work with death. I work with life."

She went on to tell him the different ways she had helped people over the years, in many different capacities. Then she confided that of all the places she had been, there was more life behind that picture window than in any other situation she had ever experienced.

"It's a different world in that room," she said. "Every moment is precious; nothing is taken for granted. It's a world that has no time for bitterness and grudges. People aren't afraid of their feelings. If they want to laugh, they do it right out loud. If they want to cry, they go ahead and do it. And when they cry, they never cry alone, because there is always someone to hold them.

"It's a world where people forgive, because life is too precious to waste raging against others. It's a world where people take care of one another. And when some of those children have enough strength to

get out of bed, do you know what they do?
They go to comfort a child who is less
fortunate."

She paused, and when she looked at the
man her face seemed to be glowing, "I
work with life," she repeated firmly.[1]

God used that article to make an attitude adjustment
in my life at a time when it needed serious adjustment.
It forced me to reacquaint myself with the Biblical
concept of "living one day at a time" in a fresh, new way.
Soon after, I began asking myself a series of questions
each morning when dawn broke and my day began:
"Today, Sharon, could be the last day of your life. How
are you going to spend it? What kind of attitude will
you have? What kind of words will you use? What kind
of person will you be?"

I cannot begin to tell you how this one exercise has
transformed my life, not only as a person but also as a
mother. It has changed or, perhaps I should say,
corrected my sometimes ungrateful and discontent spirit.
It has motivated me to redefine my priorities by focusing
my energy, strength, and my abilities on today and not
on the promise of tomorrow. It has made me more

mindful of the preciousness of each moment and the importance of taking nothing and no one for granted.

Too often, we transfix our thoughts on what has happened in the past or what may happen in the future. Seldom do we give our full allegiance to what is at hand – the present. When I shared this story with a doctor friend of mine, she suggested I also read a book written about children with cancer by Erma Bombeck called, *I Want To Grow Hair, I Want To Grow Up, I Want to Go To Boise*.

As I read each chapter, I was struck by how similar the nun's words were to the attitudes of these young people. Probably the most significant similarity I discovered was their attitude about today. Their suddenly shortened lives had given them the gift of cutting through the "what ifs," "what should have been," "what might be" and allowed them to bask in the "what is now." They had unearthed a deep desire within themselves to make the most of the time given them. With no promise of a future, they had learned to live each day to the fullest.

Erma tells the story of a young boy with a brain tumor who loved to draw. One day he was asked the question, "Are you going to be an artist when you grow up?"

Indignantly he replied, "I am an artist."[2] He understood something you and I sometimes miss. There may not be a tomorrow.

Let me ask you: Do you view life from this perspective? Are you seizing the day? Are you basking in each moment? I believe each one of us needs to get better at cutting through the jungle of the "what ifs," "what should have been," "what might be" and breathe in the exhilarating scent of "what is now."

Do you know what would happen if you really believed that today would be the last day you would spend with your children? You'd be a different mother.

❖ You wouldn't use your child for target practice when you were emotionally overwhelmed. Personal struggles and internal frustrations would be laid at the feet of Jesus and not on the psyches of your child.

❖ You wouldn't allow your attitude to be infiltrated with such negative emotions as anger, disappointment, or irritation on a regular basis. Rather, your demeanor would be sprinkled with seeds of kindness, patience, and gentleness.

❖ You would realize that your child is a wonderful gift from God that has been entrusted to you to nurture, to teach, and to protect. You would lead by example. You would discipline with love. You would pray without ceasing.

❖ You would be more fun to live with. You would smile more. The sound of your laughter would float through your home like a scented candle.

❖ You would be a good listener. You wouldn't be too tired to listen to the dreams, concerns, and complaints of your child. You would refrain from becoming impatient at his/her tendency to interrupt.

❖ You would speak the truth with love. You would say those things that needed saying but without criticism, sarcasm, and threats. You would be more interested in recon-ciliation and compromise than in doing things your way.

❖ You would love more. You would love with the best of who you are, not half-heartedly or with strings attached. You wouldn't miss an opportunity to tell your child, both in words and actions, what a treasure he or she is in your life.

My friend, you would be a different mother!

Children have never
been good
at listening
to their elders,
but they have
never failed
to imitate them.

James Baldwin

More is Caught than Taught

I am a fruitcake fanatic. I'm not kidding. I make a fruitcake for myself every Christmas and methodically eat it for breakfast, lunch, and supper until every last morsel is gone. It has become one of those delectable traditions of my life. In a two-week period I gain approximately five to ten pounds. I should be ashamed of my lack of self-control, but I can honestly say that the taste of fruitcake with a cup of coffee is worth fifty weeks of low fat and zero sugar.

I hate to share my fruitcake, too. When my mother didn't come for Christmas one year, I had the audacity to call her and say, "The only good thing about your staying in Minnesota is that I get the fruitcake all to myself." One day in a moment of weakness, while I was sitting at the kitchen table eating my fifth helping of fruitcake for the day, I said to my youngest son, Brad, "Would you like to have some fruitcake?"

Now I would never have asked any of my older children that question because they had made it clear to me through the years that they "hated" fruitcake. "How can you eat that stuff?" they would snarl with disgust. He was the last of my children I had any hope of converting.

"No thanks," he responded with a look that conveyed serious questions about my mental stability.

"Have you ever tried fruitcake?" I demanded.

"No," he groaned incredulously.

"Well then, how do you know you don't like it?" I pressed.

"Because everyone in the family hates fruitcake so I hate fruitcake, too!" he said with conviction.

I am absolutely sure no one in our home had ever sat Brad down to give him a formal lesson on the perils of eating fruitcake. Yet Brad knew beyond a shadow of a doubt that he hated it! Why? Because he had listened to his sisters and brother. Their words of condemnation directly affected his opinion about fruitcake. Though humorous, I admit, this anecdote illustrates a powerful truth that has come down through the ages of parenting: more is caught than taught!

As mothers, it is important that we ask ourselves often what our words, and what our actions are saying to our children. Are they about such things as excellence, sincerity, persistence, kindness, and forgiveness? I read a quote some time ago that reaffirms the tremendous impact our behavior has on our offspring: "Children are constantly watching their parents, listening to what they say to each other and checking to see if words and deeds match."[1] One of the most valuable gifts you can give your child is a good example.

I'm sure you are familiar with the Biblical story of Daniel and the lions' den. What some of us don't realize is that Daniel had made quite a name for himself long before God delivered him from the king of beasts. Two verses in the Book of Daniel speak loudly about the reputation he had built among his contemporaries.

> "Now Daniel so distinguished himself among the administrators and satraps by his exceptional qualities that the king planned to set him over the whole kingdom." (6:3)

"...They could not find any corruption in him because he was trustworthy and neither corrupt nor negligent." (6:4)

It was his words and his actions that distinguished him. It was his qualities. It was the way he lived them out in everyday life.

What kind of character have you built as a mother? Do your children see honesty, integrity, and decency in action in your life? Do they witness confidentiality, self-discipline and loyalty day in and day out? Children cannot mimic what they do not see. Our lives must be an open book where they can read with clarity the importance of being enthusiastic...avoiding sarcastic remarks...showing respect...taking responsibility for ourselves and not blaming others...keeping promises...being courteous...complimenting others...being brave...leaving criticism at the back door...being fair...keeping a secret ...being loyal...not gossiping...being punctual...being thankful...being forgiving...being tenderhearted...saying you're sorry...appreciating others...not carrying a grudge ...being a good listener...being tactful...not whining... laughing a lot...being kind...and above all, being loving.

The power behind our actions was driven home to me a few years ago at a large conference I attended. The speaker was telling the story of watching her daughter crack an egg for the first time. The young girl did not use two hands like most "new cooks" would have done. She used just one hand. She used the same hand her mother always used. The true significance of this seemingly small incident, you see, was that her mother only had one hand.

She had imitated her mother. And your children will, whether you like it or not, imitate you as well. Will you like what you see? These are tough questions, but they are worth asking.

My friend, lead your children by example. Remember...more is caught than taught.

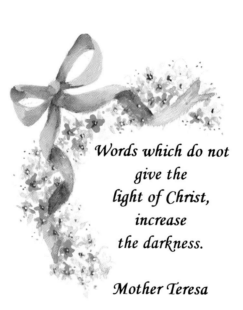

Words which do not
give the
light of Christ,
increase
the darkness.

Mother Teresa

The Power of Your Words

My father was a man of few words. Those he chose to deliver were spoken with unquestionable authority. He had the knack of being convincing, commanding, even forceful in a matter of minutes with just a handful of sentences. As a child, I remember being captivated by his views and perceptions of life. I recall listening carefully to each and every one of his instructions. My memory can easily pull up dozens of scenarios where I quietly listened to his parental advice. I was like a little sponge soaking up the water of his knowledge and experience. He had a great influence on my life for a very long time.

Unfortunately, not all his concise and calculated words were helpful or of benefit to me. Sometimes they were hurtful and harsh. Many times, whenever he became frustrated with my behavior, he would resort to calling me "names" as a means of changing me. These less than complimentary names would cut deep into my heart. The phrase I remember hearing the most was "you are so selfish." He used it on a regular basis. It is a label I have tried desperately to erase for years.

To this day, I would do just about anything not to be thought of or characterized as a selfish person. Besides my faith, I believe my tremendous need to give to those I love and to the world around me is prompted by my inner desire to prove my father wrong. Please understand, I do not believe for one second that my father ever meant to hurt me. In his zeal to make me a better person, he falsely believed that negative reinforcement would achieve the goal he was looking for. I use this example of my father advisedly. I have no desire to blemish his memory. I use it only as an illustration to help myself and others learn from his "sincere" mistake. Even though they were unintentional, his words hurt me then and, in a small way, still hurt me today.

Sadly enough, history has repeated itself. I heard those same words again this year. This time they were the echo of my own voice. They were relayed to me by one of my daughters. She had been telling me about an incident that had occurred between her and her brother. "Mom," she said, "I know I can be too possessive with my things. I remember your telling me that when I was a child. You said I was selfish." Her words penetrated me like a knife. I had said to her what my father had said to me. I had mimicked him, even if unknowingly.

Do I consciously remember saying those things to my daughter? No. Did I say them? Yes. I can only suppose that at the time I probably never gave my words a second thought. I probably rationalized that this was just one of those things that a parent says to a child. I know for sure I never imagined her being able to recall them at age 20. You see, what I didn't realize then, along with so many other parents before me, was how powerful my words are in the life of my child.

Do you see your words having that kind of influence? Are you aware that just a handful of nouns and verbs can make a difference between a smile and a tear? Or have you allowed yourself to be subtly coaxed into believing that what you say has little consequence? That what comes forth from your mouth really doesn't matter?

Solomon, in the Book of Proverbs, used some pretty strong language about the impact our words have on others.

"Reckless words pierce like a sword but the tongue of the wise brings healing." (12:18)

"He who guards his lips guards his life, but he who speaks rashly will come to ruin." (13:3)

Allow me to translate these for you as a mother. Cutting and off-the-cuff remarks will cause your child inner pain, but thoughtful, caring words will bring him comfort and encouragement. Words, once spoken, make an indelible mark.

None of us would ever disagree with this, yet sometimes, in the midst of dirty houses, frustrating relationships or unending demands, we sometimes forget how far-reaching our words really are. Years ago, my daughter Katy returned from a youth retreat and shared with me a three-question formula she had learned in relation to weighing one's words that has stayed with me to this day.

Before she spoke or responded to another person, she was to ask herself three questions: Is it kind? Is it true? Is it necessary? And if she couldn't answer "yes" to all three questions, then she probably shouldn't say it. This has proven to be a wonderful litmus test for me personally, and I would challenge you to use it as well. Is what you are about to say kind? Is what you are about to say true? Is what you are about to say necessary? This is one way of guarding yourself against verbal recklessness.

Now this is not to say I shouldn't have confronted my daughter about her tendency to be too possessive with her belongings. The need to teach, correct, and admonish a child is a constant that should never be neglected, especially during those impressionable years. The reproof itself was not my sin. It was the negative way I delivered it. I should have separated the person from the behavior. Instead of calling her a "selfish person," I should have called her behavior "selfish." That one distinction would have made all the difference.

Mothers, you will never fully know the effect your words will have on your child but you can be sure of one thing, they *will* have an effect. They will either lift up or tear down. They will either bring joy or pain. They will encourage or discourage, inspire or reject. The choice is up to you.

The mother's heart
is the
child's
classroom.

Henry Ward Beecher

Mothering –
A Perpetual Balancing Act

I am a New Englander born and bred. I love where I live not only because of the beautiful countryside but also because of the deep roots that exist between family and friends. I moved away once a long time ago but the longing to return was a constant that never left me. It was a yearning born out of an old adage we toss around here repeatedly – "Once a New Englander...always a New Englander." I found my way back almost seventeen years ago now, but I did so with a heightened sense of appreciation for my Yankee heritage, history, and culture.

In the vast showcase of historical gems in the New England area is Newport, a tiny seaport on the coastline of Rhode Island. It is home to some of the most spectacular summer homes that were built during the Gilded Age. One of its most impressive mansions is called the Marble House which was built in the late 1800's by the Vanderbilt family. We are told that when the family was in residence each summer, it took a staff of 36 to care for the property – 23 indoor and 13 outdoor servants.

Today, a single caretaker along with a small cleaning staff maintains this 50-room period estate where they reside. Each day they wipe down the floors of each room, and twice a month they wax them. They vacuum the rugs daily and dust the rooms every other day. And this is just for starters! The upkeep of this opulent dwelling is an enormous task to say the least.

I learned about these preservation details from an article I read entitled "Cleaning the Castle." It was an informative essay on the challenges of picking up after hundreds of tourists on a regular basis. Halfway through the article, I found myself wondering why anyone would want to go to all this work to keep a house clean? Why would anyone want to do the same thing day in and day out, year in and year out? The answer came in short order and straight from the horse's mouth.

"This is not my house," the caretaker explained, "but it is my home."[1]

I now had my answer. He had hit the nail squarely on the head. A house is a building. A home is a sanctuary. A house is filled with furniture. A home is filled with love. A house is for lodging. A home is for caring. The caretaker understood the difference between the two. He had learned to embrace each task with the end result in mind. Ultimately, he knew that the business of preserving a home was far more important than maintaining a house.

Most mothers worth their weight in gold know the difference as well. Their struggle is not a lack of knowledge but of focus and consistency. They know the right way. They just forget to live it out once in a while. And it is no wonder given the array of demands and expectations they are handed on a daily basis. Their rough and tumble world of non-stop living provides an innocuous breeding ground for blurring the lines between being a caretaker of a soul and a janitor of things. It is easy to do. I know. I've done it.

I can't help but wonder how many times I got so caught up in the demands of cooking, cleaning, and coordinating that I forgot about the importance of nurturing, protecting, and teaching those entrusted to my care. I wonder how many times I allowed myself to become a tour director of activity instead of an imparter of emotional, mental, and spiritual nourishment to my precious children. Though my intentions were no doubt pure, I know there were moments when my priorities were clearly out of order, when I majored in minor things, or when the emphasis was on the wrong syllable.

Since I know you grapple with these same issues, may I offer you this gentle reminder today about your calling as a mother. You are a "gardener planting seeds of faith, truth, and love that develop into the fairest flowers of character, virtue, and happiness in the lives of your children."[2] The greatest gifts you have to give are those that come from your heart. They are a sense of worth and value, a foundation of support and encouragement, and a fortress of security and stability. Try not to let the sheer force of life tinker with your sense of balance. Don't get sidetracked with secondary issues. Remember, there is a world of difference between preserving a home and maintaining a house. Just ask the caretaker.

"There is a time to show my child...God in earth and sky and flower, to teach him to wonder and reverence.

There is a time to leave the dishes, to swing him in the park, to run a race, to draw a picture, to catch a butterfly, to give him happy comradeship.

There is a time to point the way, to teach his infant lips to pray. To teach his heart to love God's Word, to love God's day...for children don't wait.

There is a time to share with him my best in attitudes – a love of life, a love of God, a love of family.

There is a time to answer his questions, all his questions, because there may come a time when he will not want my answers.

There is a time to watch him bravely go to school, to miss him underfoot.

There is a time to teach him independence, responsibility, self-reliance, to be firm but friendly, to discipline with love.

For soon, so soon, there will be a time to let him go, the apron strings untied...for children won't wait.

There is a time to treasure every fleeting moment of his childhood... the precious ears to inspire and train. A time to understand that an hour of concern today may save years of heartache tomorrow.

The house will wait, the dishes will wait, the new room will wait... but children don't wait."

Excerpt from Helen Young's poem, "Children Won't Wait"

*A child's mind
is like a
bank -
whatever you put in,
you get back
in ten years -
with
interest.*

Frederic Wertham

Breeding –
A Forgotten Word

Not long ago, I was involved in a conversation with a friend that centered around the manners or, I should say, lack of manners of young people today. "They don't seem to have the kind of breeding we were given as children," she remarked. When our discussion ended, I found myself intrigued with the word she used – "breeding." Of course, I knew what it meant. I just hadn't heard it for a long time. Evidently it, along with the virtues of honesty, integrity, and civility had been put out to pasture in our wonderfully enlightened society (with tongue-in-cheek I write these words).

It's really not a bad word though. In fact, it is rich in meaning. To breed a child means to teach him the difference between right and wrong, good and bad, and acceptable and unacceptable behavior. Its purpose is to instill a foundation of moral definitives. Its guiding principle is to lead a child to a lifetime road of strong character development.

Parents are, without a doubt, the primary breeders of their children. Their influence in this whole area of child-rearing is enormous, to say the least. The discipline they offer is an invaluable part of the nurturing process. Do you know what the word "discipline" actually means? It comes from the Latin root meaning "to teach." It has to do with teaching a child what behavior is acceptable. The right kind of discipline should take place all the time, 24 hours a day. It not only involves setting boundaries but reacting to bad behavior as well. Discipline and punishment are really two different things. Discipline means teaching your children what to do and how to control their behavior. Punishment is imposing a consequence for wrong, bad or unacceptable behavior.

Unfortunately, there are too many children today dying of moral neglect at the hands of parents who don't want this kind of responsibility, and who don't want to make the tough choices. They want to be their child's friend, not a parent. There is a time for a parent to be a child's friend but it is not when the child is young and in need of the kind of supervision that requires the use of the word "no." The kind of supervision that issues boundaries and makes children accountable for their actions.

I know this is true, not because I read newspapers, magazines, and books, but because I have raised six children of my own and can see the multiple changes that have taken place over the past 20 years. Do you know that last year was the first time I have ever had one of my children's friends speak to me disrespectfully. I was baby-sitting a friend of Brad's at the time. When things began to get boring at our house, Brad and his friend went down the street in hopes of hooking up with some kids from the neighborhood. They were gone longer than I expected.

Wanting to assure myself that everything was all right, I left the house and headed down the street only to find Brad's friend headed straight my way. "Scott," I called out, "where's Brad?"

Angrily, he shouted back, "He's at Robert's house. He ditched me to play with the other kids. I'm going back to the house, get my Sega tape and I'm out of here."

"Scott," I responded, "you can't leave. I'm baby-sitting for you."

Without missing a beat, he walked right past me and said, "Wanna bet?"

I was shocked to say the least but recovered quickly enough to say, "Young man, you are to stop right where you are and turn around and look at me." He did as I asked. His body language twisted in defiance. "I don't know what kind of trouble you are having with my son, but I want to make something very clear to you. You are never to talk to me that way again. You are to treat me with respect. Do you understand? I would like you to apologize for the way you just acted."

Of one thing I am very sure: this was not the first time this young man had behaved in this manner. He had been allowed to speak and act that way long before he met me.

The Book of Proverbs says, "If you love your children, you will correct them..."[1] In an atmosphere void of discipline and punishment, you will find kids with knives, guns, and attitudes. Kids who are out of control. Children need and want limits, boundaries, rules, and structure. They gain security from them. It conveys the message that someone cares about them and what they will become. As much as they resist, balk, and complain, children are inwardly hoping their parents use the weight they carry.

Give your child the training he deserves. Teach him the principles of good behavior. Be about the business of strong character building. Issue boundaries. Be consistent with your warnings and make your child accountable for his actions.

I love old books. I love to read the thoughts of others who have gone before me. A few years ago in an antique shop in Connecticut, I found a wonderful gem that was written in 1880 called *Home and Health*. Much of its contents would seem archaic by today's standards, but some of it I found highly enriching. It taught basic rules of behavior and civility that has become lost in our "do whatever feels good" society. It touched on everything from parenting skills to hints and helps in conversation.

One section I found particularly interesting was entitled "Family Government: Forty-two Hints" and it began with these words:

> "Family Government is to be family government. It uses authority, authority in love, yet authority.

It ordains law.   It commands the
child's moral nature."[2]

My friend, that is what breeding is all about.   Its
thoughtful and consistent instruction is an invaluable
asset to a child.   I think the art of breeding needs to make
a comeback.   Don't you agree?

The most wasted
of all days
is that
on which
one has not
laughed.

Anonymous

Spotlight on Laughter

My younger son, Bradley and I were driving to the ball field one day for his first spring practice. Since I knew I had a captive audience, I used the driving time to lecture him on something he had done wrong that afternoon. My colorful spiel went on and on with nary a word from my passenger. After a few moments of silence, he turned to me and dryly said, "And your point is?" If there had been tension in the car at that point, it excused itself when the laughter began. I completely lost it, much to my son's delight.

My older son, Brian was watching television in our family room one day while he was in high school. When I saw him sitting there, I began to lecture him on the state of his room. "Brian," I said, "your room is in such bad shape that if anyone went in there, they might not be able to find their way out. You could be indicted for involuntary asphyxiation!" Like his brother, he never said a word.

When I finally finished, he calmly looked down at the dog sitting at his feet, looked back up at me, looked back down at our "giant" 8 lb. dog and called out, "Sic her!" If there had been tension in the room before this moment, it excused itself when the laughter began. Again I lost it, much to my son's delight.

May I ask you a question? When you read these amusing anecdotes, did they bring a smile to your face? Did they make you laugh? I hope so because too often, when women become mothers, they lose their sense of humor. The muscles in their faces freeze. No hint of a belly laugh let alone a smile. Everything becomes so serious. Everything is earth shattering. They get so wrapped up in wanting to do the right thing or in getting everything done that they forget the importance of laughing with their children. I mean really laughing, really being silly.

Years ago I came across an article entitled "If I Were Starting My Family Again" which was written by a father of five in response to this question: "If I could relive the years when my children were growing up, what would I do differently, knowing what I know now?" Not surprisingly, one of his top ten insights involved the need to laugh more with his children. He wrote these words, "...Oscar Wilde wrote, 'The best way to make children good is to make them happy.' I remember when I laughed with my children at the humorous plays they put on for the family, at the funny stories they shared from school, at the times I fell for their tricks and catch questions...I remember the times they told of funny experiences the family had years later, and I know it was the happy experiences which are remembered and still bind us together."[1]

I wholeheartedly concur. Especially after listening to my own adult children. Their very best memories are the ones where we laughed together as a family. Unfortunately, in our fast-paced and stressed-out world, moments of unabandoned laughter are becoming all too rare. Whenever I speak to an audience of mothers, I crusade hard about the importance of becoming mothers who are fun to live with. Mothers who make their homes a fun place to be.

I tell them a story about Brad when he was six years old. It makes me laugh when I recall it, even now. It was suppertime in our house, and I had just finished cooking a pot of ziti on the stove. Brad was standing at the far end of the kitchen as I poured the ziti into a colander to drain. I honestly don't know what came over me, but I picked up a piece of warm ziti and hurled it in Brad's direction. In case you don't know, warm ziti sticks to anything.

My aim has never been my strongest suit, but this time, I was right on the money. The small piece of limp pasta stuck firmly to Brad's chest. You should have seen the look on his face. He was absolutely shocked. Of course, you know what he did next. He threw it right back at me. So I returned fire. There we were, a crazed mother and son running around the kitchen battling each other with ziti. We were laughing so hard we could hardly catch our breath! Crazy? Certifiably to be sure. But you know what? We had fun. I want my children to remember me as a mother who laughed with them.

We have been doing something in our home each night that has helped bring laughter, as well as good conversation, into our dinnertime hour. Perhaps you could try it in your home. Each person sitting at the table has to answer three questions: What was the best thing that happened to you today? What was the worst thing that happened to you today? And what was the funniest thing that happened to you today? A number of good chuckles have been had over the animated stories that have graced our table.

Give it a try. Its possibilities are endless. You might even hear about the girl in your son's fourth grade class whose brightly designed underwear could be seen through her white stretch pants!

Do you know what "momisms" are? They are well worn phrases used by mothers the world over. You probably heard them from your mother and she heard them from her mother and your children will hear them from you. Do you recognize any of these vintage "momisms?"

- ❖ Always wear clean underwear in case you are in an accident.
- ❖ Do you think I am made of money?
- ❖ I'm not *asking* you. I'm *telling* you.
- ❖ If you don't stop doing that, your face will freeze that way.
- ❖ If I talked to my mother the way you talk to me...
- ❖ Close the door behind you. You weren't brought up in a barn.

Did I get you to smile? I hope so. My desire has been to remind you that laughter really is the best medicine. And to encourage you to laugh more, laugh longer, and laugh harder with your children. Let laughter fill your home like a warm, scented candle. It will bring the best of memories!

Legacies
are gifts
from the heart
and
insights
from the soul.

Sharon Anderson

A Mother's Legacy

"You have your mother's hands," my daughter Christy remarked as she watched me paint my nails. I looked at them as if for the first time, and was struck by how similar our hands really were. This was yet another one of my features that closely resembles my mother. It seems these similarities become more pronounced the older I get. Since she is one attractive lady, I am thankful to have inherited some of her genes.

However, the gratitude I feel most towards my mother comes not out of her genetics, but out of her character. The influence she has had upon my life has little to do with her appearance and everything to do with her presence. It was the way I watched her live, the things I heard her say, the lessons she sought to teach, that marked her legacy to me as her daughter.

I was once asked the question, "What one lesson did your mother teach you as a child that has stayed with you to this day?" My answer came quickly. It had been so deeply ingrained within me for years that it took no thought at all. "Sharon," she would say to me whenever I faced a childhood crisis, "if you can do something about this, then do it; if you can't, then let it go." This rich piece of wisdom has affected my life in profound ways over the years. In fact, it has followed me throughout my adult life as I've dealt with the multiple issues of personal responsibility. It has also helped me find the courage and freedom to release those things that are beyond my control.

Another choice snippet I heard often came straight from the Bible. She recited it often. "Sharon," she would say, "to whom much is given, much is required."[1] These words have played a resonant chord within my soul for as long as I can remember. The crux of its message has motivated many of my decisions to give of myself to the world around me. What she had wanted to impart to me was a deep consciousness of being accountable for the gifts God had given to me.

To her credit, these are just some of the valuable legacies she has passed down to me through the years. It has taken hindsight and age for me to appreciate their true value. What I'm hoping is that when my children are older, they, too, will be able to look back and cherish some of the legacies I sought to pass down to them as well. Legacies of spiritual truths, moral values, and insights for everyday living. My greatest desire, barring none, is that they will inherit a hunger for God, a love of life, and a heart of compassion.

Have you given much thought to the legacy you are handing down to your own children? Do you have a full understanding of the kind of influence you have in their lives right now? Are you living in the present with the future in mind when it comes to passing on your values, your morals, and your own special kind of wisdom? My friend, legacies are gifts from the heart and insights of the soul. What you pass down today will be heirlooms for tomorrow.

I have a friend who is a Hospice volunteer. She is a loving, caring woman who becomes very involved in the lives of the terminally ill she cares for. One of her assignments involved a 42-year-old Haitian woman dying of cancer. It seemed the woman had only one child, a 12-year-old daughter. Her name was Myrdell.

She and her mother had lived alone for years, so their relationship was an unusually close and intimate one. As death approached, Myrdell wrote a poem about her mother that was later read at the funeral. Even at a very young age, this young woman had received her mother's legacy in full measure. Here are some thought-provoking excerpts from this amazing tribute. May it be a model for us all.

> "Lord, grant me the strength that you granted my mother so I might be able to endure life's hardships *'even more'*
>
> Lord, grant me the calmness that you granted my mother so that I might be able to know you are in control *'even more'*
>
> Lord, grant me the joy that you granted my mother so that I might be able to 'rejoice in the Lord always' *'even more'*

Lord, grant me the love that you granted my mother so that I might be able to give up all I have for someone in need and love my future children as she loved me *'even more'*

Lord, grant me the knowledge of others that you granted my mother so that I might be able to treat them properly *'even more'*

Lord, grant me the friendliness that you granted my mother so that people might be able to see in me your light *'even more'*

Lord, grant me the wisdom that you granted my mother so that I might be free from foolish mistakes and be obedient to your perfect will *'even more'*...

Lord, grant me the beauty that you granted my mother so that I might be called an angel of God *'even more'*...

Lord, grant me the child-like behavior that you granted my

mother even in her adult years so that I might be able to "have fun" no matter how old I am *'even more'*...

Lord, grant me the closeness of you that you granted my mother so that I might be able to also lead others to a close walk with God *'even more'*

Lord, grant me the laughter that you granted my mother so that I might be able to pass the cloud of hard times with a smile *'even more'*

Lord, grant me the privilege to be just like my mother who was a wonderful model for all Christian women *'even more.'"*[2]

Myrdell Belizaire, 1998

The only thing
of value
we can give
our kids
is what
we are,
not
what we have.

Leo Buscaglia

One-Hour Vacations

As I reflect over my child-rearing years with my older children, I have come to the humbling conclusion that I made a huge mistake! Not an intentional one, mind you, but an erroneous one nevertheless. A faux pas I see being repeated by mothers all around me during those prime time years of nurturing.

My blunder? I seldom took time for myself in the midst of the journey. I know this statement probably sounds heretical when mirrored against the sacred oath of motherhood, but I assure you that its logic is sound and its benefits are measurable. Hindsight has been kind enough to show me the error of my ways and beckons me to pass on this tidbit of wisdom.

When I first became a mother, and for subsequent years afterwards, I adhered to the faulty notion that motherhood was a "sunup to sundown" tour of duty where all future leaves were hereby canceled. I saw myself as the helmsman of the ship, and everyone knew the helmsman never left her post. She was expected to be on deck through wind, sleet, and rain...without a break! So for me that meant cleaning the bathrooms without a break. Reading books to little ones without a break. Taxiing children around without a break.

Somehow I, along with thousands of other mothers, innocently believed that taking time for myself was somehow selfish and self-centered. Caring for my own soul and body was indulgent, if not selfish. I rationalized that sabbaticals were only for professors and preachers, certainly not for mothers. I further justified this behavior with the sound argument that my children needed me. "No," I would say to myself, "quality time doesn't take the place of quantity of time no matter what the media is telling me."

Ladies, it has taken me years to see how very wrong I was. I have learned that good mothering, healthy mothering involves taking good care of yourself as well as your children. It is about taking time regularly for refreshment and restoration.   It is about what I call taking regular one-hour vacations.

Let me ask you. When was the last time you called a "time-out" for yourself? When was the last time you walked away from the demands of your home for an hour and did something you find relaxing and invigorating? I would dare say for many of you, it has been quite a while. I learned the benefits of these one-hour vacations quite by accident when my youngest child was in kindergarten.

It was April school vacation in our area of the country and my five-year-old son, Bradley had asked to have a friend over for the day since all his siblings had made other plans. I agreed to his request and soon he and his friend Spencer were involved in the wonderful world of make believe.

While the boys were out playing, I took advantage of the quiet by cleaning out some neglected closets. In the midst of this spruce-up detail, I came across a kite I had bought Brad eons ago. Like all efficient mothers, I had put it away for the future and had then forgotten where I had hidden it!

Since it was a warm and windy day, I took the kite outside and asked the boys if they wanted to help me fly it. Their enthusiastic response paved the way for what would be an unexpected and surprising adventure. Before I go on, I must tell you that it had been years since I had flown a kite, so it took me a while to figure out how to maneuver the kite and the strings in tandem. In fact, it took a good long while.

There we were, a mother and two five-year-olds huffing and puffing our way across the yard, desperately hoping that the wind would catch our new kite. Each time we would get it eight to ten feet in the air, it would do a grand free-fall back to earth with the speed of light. We didn't give up though.

We kept at it until that magical moment when our little kite took flight. It was so exhilarating to watch that sky bird hurl its way across the bright, blue sky. The higher the kite went, the more excited I became. In fact, I was so engrossed in the moment that I never realized that I was flying the kite alone! The boys had long since taken their leave.

I remember wondering at that moment what people driving by my yard must have been thinking, especially those who knew me. Here I was, a grown woman, flying a kite all by myself in the middle of the day. A woman who should have been cleaning a house, doing some laundry, making a bed, anything but flying a kite. But, you know, I was having so much fun that I made the decision to stay out in that field for more than an hour. I felt like a kid all over again. It was like breathing a breath of fresh air.

I walked back inside the house that day a different mother. I felt refreshed and ready to tackle the mounds of dirty laundry before me with a renewed sense of vigor. All it took was an hour. A brief sixty-minute reprieve away from the demands, decisions, and difficulties of everyday life.

Mothers, I urge you to join me in making one-hour vacations a regular part of your busy lives. You are a hardy lot to be sure, but you are not an infallible one. Your minds, your emotions, and your bodies need to be taken care of so you, in turn, can take better care of those children entrusted to your care. You cannot give out what you do not take in. You cannot give the best of who you are when you are emotionally, physically, and mentally on overload.

One-hour vacations will help you keep your per-spective. They will help you appreciate that which is yours. They will slow you down and help you to remember what is really important. They will enable you to be more of the mother God has called you to be.

"...This time away from the hubbub of everyday living has been good for me. It has given me time to reflect. Time to reassess where I'm going and what things in my life need improvement. It also makes me thankful for my life, my family, my friends, and my work. By walking away even if for this hour, I have found balance and refreshment."

Sharon Anderson, August, 1994

*Children
have more
need of
models
than of critics.*

French Proverb

Listening from the Heart

"Mom, are you listening to me?" "Mom, did you hear what I said?" "Mom, are you paying attention?" Have you ever heard those questions reverberating from your child? Of course, you have. Do you ever remember challenging your own mother in this way? Of course, you do. All children worth their mettle have from time to time called into question their parents' listening skills.

I do a fair amount of speaking to mothers' groups (six children will do it every time) and one of the areas I touch upon often is the need for mothers to become their child's Number 1 best listener. At the end of each of my sessions, I encourage the women to identify what I call their "keeper" for our time together. Their "keeper" is that *one* thing they heard me say that prompted some pangs of conviction. That *one* specific mothering skill in need of some sharpening!

I am always amazed at the number of women who without exception choose "better listening skills" as their keeper of the day. They see themselves as being quick to speak but slow to listen. Through our time together, they are able to recognize the importance of listening, really listening, not only to the concerns of a teenager, but to the chitchat of a toddler as well. I am rapidly coming to the conclusion that "half-ear" listening is one of the most unintentional sins parents commit against their children everyday.

I mentioned earlier an article I read as a young mother entitled "If I Were Starting My Family Again," that made a deep impression on me. It was written by a man who had raised five children of his own. "If I were starting my family again," he wrote, "I would be a better listener. Most of us, as parents, find it hard to listen. We are busy with the burdens of what must be done. We are often tired from a full day of responsibilities or wrapped in attention to our own interests and have little time to listen. A child's talk seems like chatter and unimportant. If my child were young again, I'd stop reading the newspaper when he wanted to talk to me. And I would try to refrain from impatience at the interruption. Such times can be the best opportunity to show love."[1]

Did you know it is estimated that the average child asks 500,000 questions by the age of 15? A half a million opportunities for a parent to share with their child the foundations of life – a love for God, a love for others, and a love for oneself. The problem most parents face is not answering the questions but hearing them. Too often they are so caught up in the rat race of everyday living that they become inattentive and sometimes insensitive to the questions stirred by childhood curiosity and adolescent arrogance.

Did you also know that listening is the foundation of all good communication and that "a relationship is as good as its communication is clear?" Good communication will not take place with your child until you have become a first-rate listener. It is an essential part of building a loving and healthy relationship. It carries with it a message of enduring worth: "I desire to know the contents of your heart."

I learned this concept first-hand years ago when my husband and I blended our families. At the time of our marriage, the ages of our children were 13, 11, 7, 6 and 5.

different conflicts, and different adjustments living under one roof! Remember the old song, "These boots were made for walking?" Well, during those early years of marriage, I rewrote those lyrics. They became "these ears were made for listening!"

I came to the quick conclusion that the only way I was ever going to be able to build any bridges in my new home was to engage the use of both my ears on a 24-7 basis, as my kids would say (translation: 24 hours a day, 7 days a week). Through this experience, I have learned four principles of good parental listening...

- ❖ It must take place all the time, not just during specified or planned moments.
- ❖ It must never begin with an agenda nor be treated with any hint of arrogance or indifference.
- ❖ It must always try to be sincere, sensitive and sympathetic.
- ❖ It must be keenly attuned to those unexpected moments when a child drops his guard and allows you entrance into his private think tank.

I would like to pass on a wonderful piece of advice I was given many years ago that helped me enormously in this whole area of listening. Whenever your child is talking to you, look directly at him! Don't look at the food you are cooking or the floor you are sweeping, but rather pivot your gaze, eye to eye, in his direction. This simple gesture communicates another powerful message: "What you think is really important to me." I found it to be the glue that kept our family's fledgling bridges from falling apart.

You will know that you are on your way to being your child's Number 1 best listener when you begin to see listening as a privilege, not as a duty.

"Can I have your mother?" is a request I sometimes get from friends less fortunate than I. They've heard about her – the hours we spend yaking in the living room, discussing future life plans, relationships, our feelings..."You can borrow her," I say, "but only for a little while. She's mine."[2]

*A mother
is a gardener
planting seeds of
faith, truth and love
that develop
into the fairest
flowers of
character,
virtue and
happiness
in the lives of
her children.*

J. Harold Gwynne

Mother with an Attitude

A survey was once done by the Census Bureau in which 3,000 employers were asked the following question: "What is the most important attribute you look for in a potential new worker whom you are deciding to hire?" Surprisingly, school grades, teacher recommendations, and employer tests were at the bottom of the list. Do you know what was at the top by a comfortable margin? Attitude!

A study was also done by a Boston geriatrician on men and women who have lived to the ripe, old age of 100. He interviewed 56 "centenarians" in his quest to discover the secrets of longevity. Do you know what he found? That a positive attitude was one of the essential keys to a long life.

As mothers, we may not be subject to the hiring standards of the work world (after all, we volunteered for this duty) or as wise as our centenarian counterparts, but we need to understand that our attitude directly impacts every area of our home. With a twist of humor my friend has a wonderful way of describing this phenomenon – "when Mama ain't happy, no one ain't happy." No truer words have ever been spoken. A mother's attitude can make or break the atmosphere of her home.

So what is this thing we call attitude and why is its impact so significant? Let me share a few things I've learned in the midst of my own journey. Attitude is a state of mind. It has to do with the way you think not only about yourself but the world around you. It is your position, your viewpoint, and your outlook on everything in life from soup to nuts.

Like character, attitude is something you choose. It is not something that just happens to you nor is it forced upon you by extenuating circumstances. It is, however, something you order. Something you control. It is a determination you make everyday of your life. Actually, when it comes to your attitude, the buck stops with you.

Sometimes we lose sight of this living in our "blame game" world where we are told nothing is our fault, where individual responsibility is replaced with the notion that we are all victims of someone else's decisions and actions. This subtle yet highly destructive thinking is affecting our society in a variety of ways, most especially in the area of personal responsibility.

Instead of making ourselves accountable for our own attitude, we are tempted to blame our husbands, our children, our economy, our friends, the mailman or even the salesclerk. As mothers, we must not allow ourselves to be deceived by this kind of thinking. We must be answerable for the attitude we display in our home.

Eight years ago our family went through an economic meltdown. It took place when my husband's business took a financial nose-dive due to factors beyond his control (a small hint: imports). Financially, we walked a fiscal tightrope that threatened our very existence. At the time, we had two children in college, three in high school and a three-year-old. Often the stress of the moment became almost intolerable as we tried to manage our threadbare checkbook. I have never ridden such an emotional roller coaster. I would go from a feeling of hopelessness to a state of numbness all in a matter of days.

In the midst of this crisis, I went away for a few days to our family's summer cottage on Cape Cod where I spent hours on the beach mulling over the details of this on-going nightmare. Something happened to me there that has since changed the way I view the intrusions and challenges of life, something that ultimately showed me that the state of my attitude was far more important than the condition of my affairs.

I'm going to let my journal tell you the rest of the story: "I'm not sure," I wrote, "what happened to me during those hours on the beach but it was as if an alarm went off in my head. I realized that I had to stop letting my circumstances affect my attitude. I had to stop feeling sorry for myself even if things weren't the way I wanted them. I had to stop drowning in my little sea of self-pity.

"For too long my attitude has lacked any kind of enthusiasm, any kind of contentment, any kind of happiness. The entire focus of my existence has been centered around what has not been happening in my life instead of on the things that were happening such as growing relationships with family members, friends and colleagues. My negative attitude was destroying me and was, no doubt, affecting those around me.

"So right there on the beach, I said out loud, 'Enough already! Stop with the negative, cranky, depressing attitude you've been nursing for so long and get back to the business of enjoying life, not just living it.'"

I can't begin to tell you the freedom I felt that day when I decided to take responsibility for my own attitude. It didn't change my circumstances, but it sure changed me. Each of us has things we wrestle with as mothers. Mine at that moment in time was finances. Yours may be a marriage that is less than fulfilling; it may be children who systemically break hearts and boundaries; it may be friends who are more self-serving than giving. Whatever it is, you are faced with the same decision I was faced with on that beach eight years ago. Are you going to let your circumstances dictate your attitude or are you going to let your attitude dictate your circumstances?

Kind words
can be
short
and
easy to speak
but their
echoes
are
truly endless.

Mother Teresa

Self-Esteem – A Tale of Two Sons

In the book *Kids Are Still Saying The Darndest Things,* children were asked the question, "What's a mom?" Some of their answers included:

- ❖ "Someone who loves you, even when you're grumpy – and even when she's grumpy."
- ❖ "A mom is the one whose gotta vacuum when the company's coming over."
- ❖ "Moms are people who make kids do stuff – like rooms and teeth."

They were also asked the question, "How would I recognize your mother if I saw her?" One gal's answer just cracked me up. "My mom has long hair that is yellow at the bottom and white in the middle and black on top!"[1]

It's scary to think of how my own children would have answered those questions years ago (I'm glad they weren't asked!). Even more revealing, however, would be how they would answer them today. No doubt, their responses would be dramatically different. And not just because of the changes that have occurred in them. I, myself, have gone through a metamorphosis of change as their mother. I have been formed and reformed, molded and remolded, fashioned and refashioned in a myriad of ways over the past two-plus decades.

Child-rearing principles have been shot at me from every angle by some pretty noteworthy sources, but I need to tell you, none have been more valuable to me than the journey itself. There is nothing like a good bit of experience to drive home a truth. Nothing like a good bit of reality to turn head knowledge into heart awareness. If only I had known then what I know now, certainly, I would have done some things differently. But since I can't go back, I was hoping you might be willing to learn from an unintentional "error in judgment" I made in my own career as a mother. It pertains to the issue of self-esteem and how it is developed in a child.

It embarrasses me to admit how utterly naive I was about this critical area of childhood development. I was always under the impression that self-esteem building was sort of like wrapping my child in a quilt of warm fuzzies on a cold winter night. It was *proactive* in nature. Something I initiated in order to make my child feel loved and of value. Sentiments such as "I love you," "I'm proud of you," or "You are special to me." Most of the time it usually meant offering positive words for positive behavior.

Curiously enough, I never understood that self-esteem building is *reactive* as well. Its goal is the same, to offer words of love and affirmation, but it is given in response to conduct that has been less than positive, to behavior that falls short of exemplary, to choices that have been poor and to boundary crossing episodes that are absolutely exasperating. I've since learned, according to the experts, that a child's self-esteem is developed by the responses he/she receives from the significant people in his/her life, whether for good or bad behavior.

Mothers, you do, without a doubt, fit snugly into the "significant" category. You are one of a handful of people who directly influences the way your child views himself. You are one of the key individuals who play a pivotal role in your child's mental and emotional development. You hold a tremendous amount of responsibility in your hands. I didn't realize how much until I was given the gift of hindsight.

I want to tell you about my two sons. They are special people to me. Their names are Brian and Brad. Brian is the older of the two. As a boy, he was always outgoing, personable, fun, but tremendously self-willed. Before the age of five, he had probably heard the word "no" spoken to him at least five thousand times and had spent half his life in a "time-out" chair (an exaggeration, of course). His motto always seemed to be "Give me liberty or give me death" and on a moments' notice could re-enact "Custer's Last Stand" with accuracy.

From the very beginning of his academic life until the age of 13, I received the same report each time I went to a teacher's conference. "He can't settle down...he doesn't focus well...he doesn't exhibit enough self-control...he gets frustrated easily," etc. Foolishly, I believed that the more his will was broken, the more control he would have over his own behavior. This poor boy was forever in trouble and, very often, for good reason. There were many times when it was difficult to respond with any sense of love and approval to this defiant and boundary jumping cowboy.

It wasn't until Brian was in seventh grade that he was diagnosed with Attention Deficit Disorder. Finally, we were able to understand the reasons behind the behavior we had witnessed for such a very long time. Finally, we were able to get him the help he needed. Sadly enough, his self-image had taken a serious beating for almost twelve years before we gained insight into his world of perpetual motion and frustration. My ignorance of his condition as well as the negative responses he had received from me over the years had taken its toll. If I could relive those years over again, my words would be filled with far more tenderness and affirmation. I had hurt someone I loved very much, even if unintentionally.

My younger son, Brad, is 12 years younger than his brother and is the youngest member of our family. He was born when the ages of his siblings were 18, 16, 12, 11, and 10. On the day he arrived, you would have thought a "Crown Prince" had been born. This child instantly knew the love of five mothers and two fathers!

He was truly loved to death! Everything he said and did during those early years was magic. I didn't realize how deeply this had affected him until he was finishing the first grade.

He had come home from school one day deeply depressed (as depressed as a first grader could be). When I asked him what was wrong, he said, "Jenna Wells doesn't like me anymore." (Jenna had been his good buddy since kindergarten.)

"Did you do something to her?" I asked.

"No," he muttered under his breath.

"Well then, how do you know she doesn't like you?" I pressed.

"She told me," he said bluntly. "She came up to me and said, 'Brad Anderson, I don't like you anymore.'"

"What did you say to her then?" I persisted.

He hesitated, thought for a moment, and then with a truly puzzled look, he said to me, "Mom, what kind of a person wouldn't like me anyway?"

You see, he had been so loved and affirmed during his short life that he couldn't imagine there being anyone in the world who wouldn't like him. What a wonderful self-image he had developed in those brief six years. Now you and I both know that Brad's self-esteem is in for some bruising as he proceeds along life's way but what a marvelous foundation he had been given. I only wish I had given Brian the same gift.

Please learn from my experience. Remind yourself often that the way you respond to your child, whether for good or bad behavior, makes a difference – a powerful difference. Hindsight has taught me this the hard way.

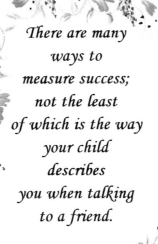

There are many
ways to
measure success;
not the least
of which is the way
your child
describes
you when talking
to a friend.

Anonymous

Do You Think
I am Pretty?

A few years ago in the church we were attending, there was a young girl by the name of Sarah who had a mad crush on my son Brad. It was absolutely the cutest thing to watch. She was enamored with him, and he was oblivious to the whole thing. She was in love. He was out to lunch. Nothing personal, mind you. As you well know, boys Brad's age don't exactly think the creation of girls was a great move on God's part.

One Sunday in early October, Sarah's parents invited our family over for dinner. When we had finished eating, Sarah was put in for a nap, and Brad, in turn, engaged in a wonderful afternoon of dirt bike riding with Sarah's father. The two-hour naptime passed quickly, and before I knew it, Sarah was standing in front of me asking where Brad had gone. After answering her question, I added, "Do you need him for something?"

"Yes," she seriously replied, "I have to ask him a question."

So once Brad came inside, I told him that Sarah had a question she wanted to ask him. He stopped what he was doing and stared at her with undivided attention. She paused a moment, perhaps gaining the courage she needed, and then finally said, "Brad, do you think I am pretty?"

I should have been touched by such childlike innocence, but I need to tell you I was spun into a near state of panic within seconds. I could only guess what Brad was thinking inside. "Pretty? Sarah, I'm not into pretty yet. Right now I think girls are a big pain in the neck." I was so afraid he was going to give some flippant, careless response that would bruise this sweet child's self-esteem.

Yet much to my surprise and delight, Brad showed a whole lot more sensitivity than I had given him credit for. "Yes, Sarah," he shyly responded, "I think you are pretty."

You should have seen the look on her face. It was priceless. He had said the magic words. Now I'm sure Sarah's parents have told her a million times that she was pretty, but Brad's words that day were golden. As I reflected over that cute incident, I was struck by the fact that outward beauty is a concern for us as women from the time we are Sarah's age to the day we die. By nature, we have a desire to look pretty, and so we should. There is nothing virtuous about letting our appearance slip into the "I don't care what I look like anymore" mode. Unkempt hair is not something we should be proud of nor are mismatched clothes a sign of modesty.

As mothers, I think we should give our appearance reasonable priority, but I also think we need to be careful not to be sucked up by the messages that are being thrown to us by our culture. A year ago I scanned the headlines of a number of women's magazines for a study I was doing and do you know what I found? A media blitz that told me "how to look younger"..."how to reclaim my youthful body"..."how to have willpower but still lose weight"..."how to do less and look better."

What I found was an idolization of outer beauty. What I didn't find was any emphasis on who we are on the inside. I saw very little credence being given to the importance of creating an attractive inner beauty that touches the lives of those around us in positive, uplifting ways. And frankly, this is a concern. I believe our society is suffering from a mindset that worships looks rather than attitude, that seems to be more concerned with what we wear than who we are. The emphasis is clearly on the wrong syllable.

The Bible says that a woman's "beauty should not come from outward adornment such as braided hair and the wearing of gold jewelry and fine clothes. Instead, it should be that of your inner self, the unfading beauty of a gentle and quiet spirit, which is of great worth in God's sight."[1] What does this mean to those of us who are knee-deep in domestic havoc and unending demands?

Let me begin by telling you what it *doesn't* mean. It doesn't mean that you shouldn't wear nice clothes. Nor is it saying that you shouldn't do your hair or should hide your jewelry in the dresser drawer. What it does mean is that you should give your highest priority to developing a beauty that shines from the inside out. A beauty that will not fade with age. A beauty that will outlive you long after you are gone!

Do you know what this kind of beauty is called? It is called your character. Do you know what your character is? It is the virtues and moral qualities that distinguish you as a person. There are three things you should know about your character. It is not something you are born with. It is not something that just happens to you. It is not dictated by circumstances. Rather, character is something you build, something you choose. You may not be able to control the world around you, but you can control what you say, what you do, and how you respond. You see, your character is the personal signature of your life.

So let me ask you a question. What kind of character have you built? What kind of habits have you established that reveal your inner beauty? What gives it its radiance? What makes your inner beauty glow? These are tough questions, but they are worth asking if you want your life to give off more light and less smoke.

On the dedication page of the very first *Chicken Soup for the Soul*, you will find these words:

> "If there is light in the soul, there
> will be beauty in the person;
> If there is beauty in the person,
> there will be harmony in the house;
> If there is harmony in the house,
> there will be order in the nation;

If there is order in the nation,
there will be peace in the world."[2]

Where does it all begin? It begins with light in the soul. What does it mean to have light in your soul? The Bible says that those who believe in Jesus will have light in their souls. Jesus said, "I am the light of the world; whoever follows me will never walk in darkness but will have the light of life."

In other words, when you believe in Jesus, you have light in your soul. This light is discovered when you invite Him into your life as your personal Lord and Savior. It is felt daily when you experience His love, peace, and hope in a very real way. "If there is light in the soul, there will be beauty in the person." Our light comes from Jesus, and it is in Him that we will find true beauty. Beauty that will not fade away. Beauty that will outlive us long after we are gone.

> "You can take no credit for beauty at 16 but if you are beautiful at 60, it will be your own soul's doing."
>
> Marie Stopes

Children are like
sponges.
They absorb
all your strength
and leave you
limp.
But give them
a squeeze
and you get it
all back.

Reader's Digest

Long Days...Short Years

I have been the mother of five teenagers so far in my life. There is one remaining child standing poised and ready to enter this pit of emotional land mines. I can't wait! These unique creatures have been an integral part of my everyday life for the past seventeen years. They have taught me lots. Much of which I now share to crowds of catatonic, trance-like mortals (parents of teenagers)!

In each of these settings I am always asked a variety of questions on how best to handle the ins and outs of adolescence. Some of the questions I am asked are good ones. Some lack common sense. Some are downright poignant. One of my favorites in the latter category is what I call a bottom line kind of question. "Of all the lessons you've learned," they ask, "what would you say is the most important one for parents of teenagers to know?"

When I was asked this for the very first time, it took me a moment to answer. Not anymore. The answer rolls off my tongue like water rolls off the back of a duck. It's a truth that is guaranteed to calm the waters of these stress-soaked relationships. It is a lesson that has been carved out in my own life one mistake at a time. It is the key to surviving the stormy days of parenthood. MAJOR IN MAJOR AND MINOR IN MINOR.

Do you know what it means to "major in major and minor in minor?" Simply speaking, it means prioritizing those things that matter and those things that do not in the relationship you build with your child. It is about making a big deal about big things and a little deal about little things. It is about establishing parameters around those issues that will be open for discussion and those that will be non-negotiable in their home during the various stages of childhood.

Years ago, there was an old saying used by men on the battlefield: "Is this hill worth dying for?" What they were asking was whether this particular skirmish was worth the ultimate price of their lives. Was this the time to fight or should they wait for a more decisive moment? In essence, that is precisely the question parents need to ask themselves often. Is this issue worth dying for in the overall scope of things?

I've seen many scenarios played out where well meaning parents majored in minor issues and the result was chaos and constant turmoil. One particular situation involved a blended family I met with whose father insisted that his new daughter (age 13) wear slippers on her feet in their new home. It seemed like a harmless enough request at first but it wasn't until I dug a little deeper that I began to understand why this had become such a hot button issue for them.

Before the mother had remarried, she and her daughter always walked around their home barefooted. A war had broken out between these individuals over what was a small, insignificant issue. This well-meaning husband and father was majoring in a minor issue, and it was threatening his relationship with his new daughter.

In fairness to this new father though, I must tell you that it is easy to put everything in the major category when you are dealing with children, especially those over the age of ten. And I also know with what result. It will be an out-and-out war on a battleground of wills. I know because I've spent a lot of time on this field.

When my oldest son was in the 8th grade, we argued every morning for the first month of school about what he was going to wear (and I mean every morning). His preference was a crummy T-shirt (and I mean crummy) and mine was a nicely pressed polo.

At some point in this 30-day war, it occurred to me that a truce needed to be called. I couldn't be fighting about T-shirts everyday when there would eventually be much bigger issues at stake. I had to "pick my battles" more carefully and much more deliberately. Now don't get me wrong. He couldn't wear whatever he wanted. He had to compromise with me and I had to compromise with him. He got to wear the T-shirt but it had to be MINUS the holes (which was his original choice). In essence, I had to learn to major in major and minor in minor.

My oldest daughter just delivered her first child. Before her son, Liam was born, she had made the decision to nurse her newborn. As with all new mothers, she had no idea to the extent with which nursing would become a full-time commitment. She, along with many of her contemporaries, was faced with an array of physical and emotional adjustments in this whole area of motherhood. She worried often about whether her son was getting enough milk since there is no way to gauge his intake level.

This concern, along with a bundle of others, was high on her list of items to discuss with her pediatrician during Liam's first check-up. The doctor assured Katy her son was indeed gaining weight and looked to be an exceptionally healthy little boy. As they concluded their conversation that afternoon, this very wise pediatrician left her with this wonderful keepsake, "Long days... short years."

No truer words have ever been said. And not just about life with an infant. But about life with a toddler, a juvenile, and an adolescent as well. Her advice captured the essence of parenthood. Long days...short years. In light of this, my friend, learn to major in major and minor in minor.

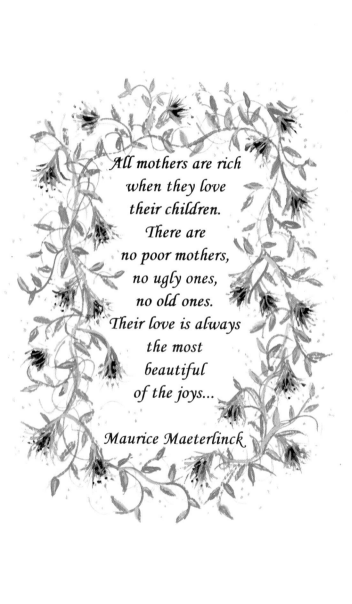

All mothers are rich
when they love
their children.
There are
no poor mothers,
no ugly ones,
no old ones.
Their love is always
the most
beautiful
of the joys...

Maurice Maeterlinck

Night Mom...Love Ya... See You in the Morning

According to a survey done on children, do you know what are the five most popular words or phrases used by mothers?

- ❖ I love you
- ❖ Yes
- ❖ Time to eat
- ❖ You can go
- ❖ You can stay up late

"I love you" took first place. How appropriate. How eternal. It seems the need to be loved is as old as time. It was as true for Adam and Eve as it is for us today. God has placed within each of us a deep longing to be loved and cherished. It's innate. It's instinctive. It's a deep-seated part of how we are wired.

For most of us, our first exposure to this type of love takes place right outside the womb. It is bestowed on us in lavish quantities by one or both parents. Dr. Marianne Neifert describes it this way: "Unconditional love, parental love, is unearned and unending. It has no strings attached, no conditions that must be met. Many of our other relationships in life depend on reciprocal benefits, but parental love is given freely to both gifted and retarded child, beautiful and blemished child, precocious and handicapped child, planned or unplanned child, boy or girl child. When delightful or obnoxious, we continue to love our child. It's the most selfless thing we ever do, sometimes the bravest thing we ever do. We love simply because it comes so naturally and because someone once did it for us."[1]

Not all children, however, are privy to this kind of love. Some suffer greatly from emotional neglect. The truth is that the love or lack of love we receive from our parents greatly influences how we see ourselves and our world. Parental love carries with it the ability to haunt us or bless us, enable us or cripple us. A study done years ago involving maladjusted teenagers confirms the indelible mark of this love. It seems that after the counselors had worked long enough to gain rapport with ten of the most maladjusted students, they were asked how long it had been since their parents had told them they loved them. Not a single one could remember having heard such a comment. By contrast, ten of the best adjusted students when asked the same question answered, "this morning" or "last night."

Let me ask you: How would your children have answered that question? Would they have said "last night" or "this morning" or would it have taken them a minute to search their memory banks? I think my own children would have needed the extra minute myself. It wasn't that I didn't love them. I love them dearly. It was just that I became so caught up with the importance of "showing" my love that I became careless about "expressing" it as well. I foolishly confused acts of love with words of love. As if one could take the place of the other.

As a speaker, I have the privilege of speaking to an array of audiences on a variety of subjects. One of my most challenging groups of listeners, as I mentioned before, is the parents of teenagers. Most of them are floating for the first time in the deep waters of puberty and can use all the help they can get.

I actually like talking about these "mutants of adolescence" because in spite of the upheaval they have caused me, I like them. I like to be around them. I used to think they should be freeze-dried at age thirteen and re-warmed at age eighteen but after raising five of them, they are starting to grow on me!

During these sessions, I offer parents a number of principles that promise to bring a degree of peace into the relationship they share with their teen; truths such as "major in major and minor in minor" and "allow your teen to try on new hats." Right in the midst of all this good hormonal advice, I bring these frazzled human beings back to the basics by reminding them of the importance of telling their teen they love them.

Within seconds, you can almost hear the moans coming from the crowd. You can almost see the eyes rolling in the back of their heads. "Come on, lady," they hiss, "we know all this. Tell us something we don't know." Tough crowd.

I take a deep breath, bite my lip and proceed with as much restraint as I can muster. "Look people, even though we all know this, it doesn't mean we are all doing this, especially when we are faced with a child we don't even like. It's one thing to say 'I love you' to a little one who is cute and obedient. It is quite another thing to say it to an abrasive adolescent who tells you that you are ruining his life. No matter how obnoxious your teen may get, he still wants and needs your love. You are important to him. Make sure he knows he is important to you." The crowd softens. They have just been given a gentle reminder of the best kind, and they know it!

For my mother's birthday one year, my youngest brother, Bob wrote a short story about a memory he had of her while he was growing up. He did the calligraphy himself and placed it in a beautiful frame along with the pictures of his three children. It hangs in my mother's home not only as a special memory of her birthday but also as a wonderful reminder that "she did something right." My brother wrote these words:

> "'Daddy, tell me a story about Memé (grandmother in French), the little child asked as he tucked her in for another night's sleep. He sat motionless for a moment, silently reflecting back to a time when time stood still. The small child waited

eagerly for another unimaginable tale that somehow proved that her Daddy was once a child, too.

He began to tell her about the house he grew up in, about walking home following a day of activity, anxiously wondering if Memé would be there. The closer he approached, the faster he walked. Hurriedly, he would climb the stone wall, cross the side lawn, scale the back stairs and push open the door and cry out, 'Mom.' Before a reply, only a mere second of silence, he felt an eternity of emptiness, but the blanket of security would cover him when he again heard the words, 'I'm in here.' The little child smiled brilliantly as she listened to her Daddy's story.

'You love, Memé, don't you, Daddy?' she asked. As a tear rolled down his cheek, he realized at that moment more clearly than ever before how much his mother truly loved him. 'Yes, I do, very much honey,' he replied. He gently kissed the child goodnight and as he reached to turn off the light, the child's soft voice called out, 'I love you, Daddy.' 'I love you, too, honey,' he responded, 'and just like Memé still loves Daddy, I will always love you.' She rolled over to dream and he walked away to remember."

This is a truth that has come down through the ages, generation after generation. We all need to be loved and we all need to be told we are loved, especially the children.

The youngest of my brood is a 12-year-old boy named Brad. Each night before he goes to bed, he comes to the door of my room and says, "Night, Mom." And then he waits for my response.

"Night, Brad," I echo.

"Love you, Mom." He lingers once again.

"Love you, too, Brad."

With eyes locked he finishes his monologue. "See you in the morning, Mom." The final pause.

"See you in the morning, Brad."

I smile. He leaves. All is well in the universe.

*I remember
my mother's prayers
and they have
always
followed me.
They have
clung to
me
all my life.*

Abraham Lincoln

A Mother's Prayer

My daughter Rachel once called me a "praying chick!" She meant it as a backhanded compliment. I took it as one of the highest she had ever given me. It is one legacy I hope she never forgets.

During the month following her son's birth, my daughter Amy called me often with the same request – "Mom, please pray that the doctors will find out what is wrong with Jacob." He had been born with an allergy in the lining of his stomach that was difficult to diagnose.

Each of my children has uttered similar words, not with a nickname but with a request – "Mom, please pray." They know the difference prayer makes, not because I told them so but because they have seen its power firsthand.

My friend, as I mentioned earlier, you can't bring your children to a place you've never been. You can't tell them to be something you are not. You can't teach them truths you refuse to live by. And you can't tell them to pray unless you, yourself, pray.

Let me ask you: Is prayer a priority in your life right now? Or has it gotten squelched out in the middle of diaper changes, dance lessons, and grocery shopping? Are you in the process of becoming a mother of prayer or are you still standing at the starting gate? Either way, I'd like to offer you this gentle reminder in the hopes that it might spur you on.

> "There is one sure test of prayer; no man can honestly engage in it and stay the way he is. His will strengthened, his pride humbled, his temper softened, his selfishness lessened, his love broadened and his courage increased. If he really prays, he will be changed. Prayer prompts forgiveness, sparks gratitude, overcomes temptation, and turns ashes of defeat into flowers of victory and fashions out of suffering

> the fragrance of triumphant love.
> Prayer is always changing things,
> never content with what is negative,
> hopeless or lost, always seeking to
> transform, to enrich, and to create.
> Prayer can become the most
> constructive force in your life."[1]

I believe this with all my heart. In fact, my passion for prayer has been part of my walk with Christ for as long as I can remember. It started when I was in high school after I read something that changed the way I viewed prayer. It made it far more personal than I had ever envisioned.

It was found in a story entitled "My Heart, Christ's Home." The narrative was about a man who had invited Jesus into his heart and then decided to give Him a personal tour of the rooms He would occupy. The room that stood out most vividly to me was the living room. It was described this way:

> "The living room was intimate
> and comfortable. I liked it. It had a
> fireplace, overstuffed chairs, a sofa
> and a quiet atmosphere. Jesus said,
> 'This is indeed a delightful room.

Let us come here often. It is secluded and quiet and we can fellowship together. I will be here every morning. Meet me here and we will start the day together.' So morning after morning, I would go downstairs to the living room and we would spend time together. These were wonderful times.

However, little by little, under the pressure of many responsibilities, I began to miss days now and then. Urgent matters would crowd out my quiet conversations with Jesus. I remember one morning rushing downstairs, eager to be on my way, when I passed the living room and saw Jesus sitting in front of the fireplace. I stopped, turned and hesitantly went in. With a downcast glance, I said, 'Master, forgive me. Have You been here all these mornings?'

'Yes,' he replied, 'I told you I would be here every morning to meet with you. Remember, I love you. I have redeemed you at a great cost. I value your fellowship.'"[2]

Through the years I've come to understand that God wants to spend time with me as much as I want to spend time with my children. Not only do I think He wants my fellowship, I think He delights in the moments I spend alone with Him.

I've also discovered that prayer is so much more than reciting a carefully scripted wish list for God. At its core, it is a friendship with the One who knows us best and loves us most. In His presence, we can tell Him the truth about our sin, our struggles, our doubts, and our fears without being judged. In the overstuffed chair, we can cry for help, ask for forgiveness and find a sense of inner peace.

A question I am asked often, especially from the mothers of young children, is how I found the time to pray when my children were little. I remember one mother confessing, "I can't seem to find the time to pray. I've tried getting up an hour before my kids do, but I find I am exhausted by the end of the day. I've tried praying at night before I go to bed, but find I'm half asleep before my head hits the pillow. I feel like a failure most of the time when it comes to my prayer life."

Sound familiar? Of course, it does. All mothers of young children (and sometimes not-so-young children) struggle with how to find time to pray in the midst of their non-stop world. After all, they are surrounded by people from morning to night. People that are either in a playpen or under their feet. People who are either in diapers or the latest fad.

So I share with them a habit I developed years ago that not only helped me create a consistent prayer life of my own but allowed me to model prayer to my children as well. Each day, depending on the most suitable time, I would announce that it was "Mom's time to talk to God." I'd ask my children to play with their toys as quietly as possible while I prayed in a chair nearby.

Naturally, when I first began this ritual, my quiet time was not so quiet. It was filled with at least fifty interruptions. But with a lot of patience and diligence, I was able to persevere and instill within my children a deep appreciation for the sacredness of this time. What I am hoping they saw was a mother who didn't just preach about prayer but lived it out as well.

I believe God used those times we spent together in front of the fire to mold me into the mother He wanted me to be. Too often, mothers think only of their prayer life as a "stand in the gap" kind of measure, a time to petition God for the needs of their children. Though this is true to a point, it should only be half of the equation. When a mother prays for her child, she should pray for herself as well. When she asks God to make changes in their lives, she should ask Him to make changes in hers as well. One prayer should not be prayed without the other.

A number of years ago now, on a cold, snowy night in January, I went to see the movie *Shadowlands* which is the love story of C.S. Lewis and his wife, Joy. I was deeply moved by this gripping story to the point where I sobbed through most of its ending. However, I was able to remember a number of poignant things that C.S. Lewis (known as Jack in the story) said about his faith in God.

One incident in particular took place after he found out his wife's cancer was in remission. His friend, Harry, a clergyman at Oxford, turned to him and said, "Jack, I know how hard you have been praying and now God is answering your prayer."

Jack turned to him and said, "That's not why I pray, Harry. I pray because I can't help myself. I pray because I am helpless. I pray because the need flows out of me all the time, waking or sleeping. *It doesn't change God, it changes me.*"

Herein lies one of the most profound truths about prayer. It doesn't change God, it changes us. Ladies, when you make prayer a priority in your life, you are giving God permission to make you into the mother He wants you to be.

*I believe in the sun
even when its
not shining;
I believe in love
even when
I am alone.
I believe in God,
even when He is silent.
Trust God
in the dark till the
light returns.*

A.W. Tozer

Please Trust Me

"I don't understand where God is sometimes in the midst of my struggles," the young mother confessed during our conversation. Her words and the sentiment behind them were not at all foreign to me. My own voice had echoed similar thoughts at different points in my own life. I remember muttering them when our finances were "maxxed out" by unexpected repairs and breakdowns. I remember groaning them when my adolescent children seemed to be more interested in challenging the rules than obeying them. I remember whispering them when my husband and I waded through one of those "less than romantic" periods of marriage. The truth is, most of us have wondered and sometimes have even been uncertain about God's role in the specific details of our lives. We have distrusted His sovereignty. We have doubted His presence. We have questioned His ways.

Lessons of hindsight have taught me that these flickerings of faith didn't take place when life dished out what I considered reasonable annoyances, but rather, when I faced a continual barrage of jarring interruptions, disagreeable attitudes, difficult decisions, and wrinkles on the faces of some of my closest relationships.

Trusting God in the light of day on the mountaintop is so easy for us to do, but it is quite another story when the way is dark and the valley is deep. It is in those moments when we find it hard to trust in a God we don't see, we don't feel and we don't understand. Satan uses these times in our lives to exploit our spiritual confusion. He tries to get us to believe that God is ambivalent to our needs and desires. It is, I have learned, one of his most poisonous and deadliest lies. Sadly enough, I must admit, I've listened to him all too often.

I don't know what you are going through today. I don't know the issues you are wrestling with or the challenges you face. But I do know one thing: you are dealing with something. Everyone is. No one has it all. It is the virtual reality of life which, my friend, brings me to my last and final reminder for the journey: Trust God. When you doubt His presence, when you ask why and when the road seems long, trust in His love. Trust in His sovereignty. Trust in His character. Trust in His Power.

"For my thoughts are not your thoughts, neither are your ways, my ways," declares the Lord. "As the heavens are higher than the earth, so are my ways higher than your ways and my thoughts than your thoughts."[1]

My friend, God doesn't make mistakes. He knows what He is doing. He has a plan in the midst of your pain and after your pain that you know nothing about. I believe that when the clouds are parted someday, you and I are going to be shocked at how God accomplished His purposes in and through our lives in a mosaic of ways. His ultimate desire is that we trust Him in the process.

A few years ago, our family planned a three-day ski trip with friends to the White Mountains of New Hampshire. Due to business demands, my husband was unable to accompany us on the trip, so my girlfriend, one of my daughters, and my youngest son Bradley, who was seven at the time, headed for the mountains one snowy night. A trip that should have taken three-and-a-half hours ended up being a six-hour saga by the time we arrived. My car couldn't make it up the mountain road where the house was located, so we hauled luggage, groceries and skis up the road by sled. By the time we finished it was two o'clock in the morning.

Of course, Brad was dying to ski the next day, so I trudged myself over to Bretton Woods to enroll him in ski school while the rest of our group went shopping. You need to understand. I am not the parent who skis with our children. My husband is the one designated for this task. I am scared to death of skiing because of an unfortunate accident I had during high school. The whole idea of going out of control and not being able to stop is absolutely frightening to me. I am what is called a stationary snow bunny. I can ski, but most of the time I try to avoid it at all costs.

On this particular day, however, the sun was shining, the weather was warm, and the view of Mt. Washington was spectacular, so I decided to ski alone after settling Brad into school. I had a fairly good day since I was able to putter my way down the mountain at my own speed, never having to worry about keeping up with anyone else. I was tired by the end of the day, but felt I had enough energy left to ski one last run with Brad when he finished ski school. Brad, of course, was confident that he could leave the bunny trial, so we headed up an intermediate trail fondly known as "Big Ben."

I should have known we were on dangerous ground when he fell down getting off the lift. It wasn't long before I realized he was in way over his head. I tried to help him the best I could, but my legs were not strong enough to hold him. My confidence level was bearing down on zero, and the pit in my stomach began to tighten. We were far from the bottom, and I wasn't at all sure how we were going to get down.

I asked a fellow skier passing by to go to the ski patrol when he got to the bottom and tell them that a mother and child were stranded at the top and needed help. We waited a while, but no one came. My knotted stomach began to do somersaults at this point because I knew by my watch that the lifts had now closed. It would be dark soon. "Take your skis off, Brad," I told him, "and just start to walk." I honestly didn't know what else to do. "Please, God," I prayed, "help us get down off this mountain."

Our journey seemed like an eternity. A first grader does not move fast in ski boots and heavy snow. We had just turned a corner when I saw a young man watching us from a ledge above. We hadn't seen any skiers for a while, so he was easy to spot. Skiing right over to us, he asked, "Do you need some help?" You can imagine my response.

"Don't worry," he said, "I've been skiing myself since I was a kid his size and I'll help you down. I'll put your son between my legs and you can follow us down. I will go real slow, so take your time. We will get to the bottom. Don't worry."

And so we began our descent. I want to tell you I was a nervous wreck as I followed this dynamic duo down the mountain. My legs were literally like putty as I snowplowed my way around each bend.

Brad's experience, however, was completely different from mine. He was having a great time. He wasn't nervous at all. After all, he was now in the hands of someone who knew exactly what he was doing. He felt the embrace of two strong arms and legs as they safely maneuvered him through each turn. He was being comforted by a soothing voice that kept saying, "You are doing just fine, Brad. Stay with me. We are almost there."

I think trusting God in the midst of life's difficulties is very much like this story. Christ is our guide. He is the One who knows what He is doing. He is the One who invites you and me to relax in His arms as He moves us through the mountains and valleys of life. He is the One who is whispering in our ears, "When you go through deep waters and great trouble, I will be with you. When you go through the rivers of difficulty, you will not drown! When you walk through the fire of oppression, you will not be burned..."[2] You see, God's love doesn't keep us from trials, it sees us through them.

The problem with you and me is that we often forget to whom we belong. We forget that there is no one like our God and that "He can do all things...no plan of His can be thwarted."[3] We forget that He promised to be "our refuge, our strength, an ever present help in times of trouble."[4] And we fail to remember that the hand that touched John 2,000 years ago with the words, "Do not be afraid. I am the First and the Last. I am the Living One..."[5] is the same one touching our lives right now. The One who told a whole nation "not to fear because He was with them"[6] is the same One who is telling you and me today "Do not be dismayed for I am your God. I will strengthen you and help you; I will uphold you with my right hand."[7]

My friend, the God who is holding the universe is the same God who is holding you right now.

Epilogue –
"Reflections of a Mother"

I have one last "reminder" for the journey. Motherhood does not come with a warranty. You could faithfully live out each and every child-raising principle outlined in this book and still not be guaranteed that your child will follow where you have led. A child is not a puppet. He is an individual who comes fully equipped with a will, personality, and temperament all his own. Your job is to love, teach, train, and nurture to the best of your ability with the help of God. The outcome of your labor ultimately rests with your child.

REFLECTIONS OF A MOTHER

I gave you life, but cannot live it for you.

I can teach you things, but I cannot make you learn.

I can give you directions, but I cannot be there to lead you.

I can allow you freedom, but I cannot account for it.

I can take you to church, but I cannot make you believe.

I can teach you right from wrong, but I cannot always decide for you.

I can buy you beautiful clothes, but I cannot make you beautiful inside.

I can offer you advice, but I cannot accept it for you.

I can give you love, but I cannot force it upon you.

I can teach you to share, but I cannot make you unselfish.

I can teach you respect, but I cannot force you to show honor.

I can advise you about friends, but cannot choose them for you.

I can advise you about sex, but I cannot keep you pure.

I can tell you the facts of life, but I cannot build your reputation.

I can tell you about drink, but I cannot say "no" for you.

I can warn you about drugs, but I cannot prevent you from using them.

I can tell you about lofty goals, but I cannot achieve them for you.

I can teach you about kindness, but I cannot force you to be gracious.

I can warn you about sins, but I cannot make you moral.

I can love you as a child, but I cannot place you in God's family.

I can pray for you, but I cannot make you walk with God.

I can teach you about Jesus, but I cannot make Jesus your Lord.

I can tell you how to live, but I cannot give you eternal life.

I can love you with unconditional love all of my life...and I will.

Author Unknown

Bibliography

Celebrate Today
1 Author Unknown
2 Erma Bombeck, I Want To Grow Hair, I Want To Grow Up, I Want To Boise (New York, NY: Harper & Row Publishers, 1989), p. 9

More is Caught than Taught
1 Author Unknown

Mothering – A Perpetual Balancing Act
1 Tina Sutton, "Cleaning the Castle" (Boston Herald, July 28, 1996)
2 J. Harold Gwynne

Breeding – A Forgotten Word
1 Proverbs 13:24 (The Promise Study Bible)
2 C.H. Fowler, W.H. DePuy, Home and Health and Home Economics (New York, NY: Phillips & Hunt, 1880), p. 24

Spotlight on Laughter
1 John Drescher, "If I Were Starting My Family Over Again" (Guideposts, 1979), p. 17

A Mother's Legacy
1 Luke 12:48b (Paraphrase)
2 "Lord, Grant Me Even More," Myrdell Belizaire

Listening from the Heart

1 John Drescher, "If I Were Starting My Family Over Again" (Guideposts, 1979), p. 17
2 Brenda Hunter, Holly Larson, In The Company Of Friends, (Sisters, Oregon: Multnomah Books, 1996), p. 81

Self-Esteem – A Tale of Two Sons

1 Dandi Daley Mackall, Kids Are Still Saying The Darndest Things (Rocklin, CA: Prima Publishing, 1994), p. 2-3

Do You Think I am Pretty?

1 1 Peter 3:3-4
2 Jack Canfield, Mark Victor Hansen, Chicken Soup For The Soul (Deerfield Beach, FL: Health Communications, 1993), p.V

Night Mom…Love Ya…See You in the Morning

1 Marianne E. Neifert, with Anne Price and Nancy Dana, Dr. Mom: A Guild To Baby and Child Care (New York, NY: Putnam's Sons, 1986), p. 11

A Mother's Prayer

1 Author Unknown
2 Robert Boyd Munger, "My Heart, Christ's Home"

Please Trust Me

1 Isaiah 55:8-9
2 Isaiah 43:2 (The Children's Living Bible)
3 Job 42:2
4 Psalms 46:1
5 Revelation 1:17
6 Isaiah 41:10
7 Ibid.

Order Form

Book - *Reminders for the Journey: Reflections for Mothers*
$15.99 plus $2.50 shipping and handling

❖   ❖   ❖

Please send me:

_____ books at $15.99 each (plus $2.50 S&H per book)

Please mail your order to:

Bridges of Hope
P.O. Box 407
South Easton, MA 02375
(508) 583-1555

Visit the Bridges of Hope web site at
www.bridgesofhope.com
for further information on additional products